Living Monsters

&

Dead Giants

By R.V. Daniels

Dedication:

This book is dedicated to God, who created all the monsters and fabulous creatures that inhabit our world.

And

This book is dedicated to children everywhere and to my own children. They taught me to see the world through the eyes of wonder.

Preface

Do you believe in monsters?

You should. They have shared our world for thousands of years.

I would like to take you on a journey of discovery. Together, we will discover a world filled with strange and mysterious creatures. Man has known and lived with monstrous creatures for many thousands of years. On our journey we will discover the monstrous beasts living in our world today and giant creatures that haunted the world of our ancestors.

There may even be monsters living close by your home. Our world is filled with strange and unusual animals and many of these living giants are on the verge of extinction due to the rapid expansion of our human world. Climate change, deforestation and pollution are pushing many species towards the brink of extinction. Invasive aliens species introduced into the ecosystems is killing off many native species.

Modern Mysteries and Prehistoric Terrors

All around our world people report seeing strange creatures. Thunderbirds, water monsters and Bigfoot regularly appear on cable television and in the pages of popular tabloid magazines. We will examine some of these monster stories and try to discover their source.

Many of the earliest sightings of these cryptids are recorded in native folktales and oral histories going back thousands of years. These early monster sightings might well be generated from actual encounters with the giant beasts from ancient times.

Come and explore a fascinating world filled with living monsters, dead giants and ancient terrors. There are many more of them than you might imagine and some are much closer to your home than you imagine. Perhaps our journey to find living monsters and dead giants will uncover the kernel of truth hidden in the monster myths and legends.

What can you do to help protect biodiversity?

As stewards of the Earth, it is the responsibility of every person to take steps to protect and conserve the natural world. It is my hope that an understanding of how these giant's live will spur people all over the world to take action and speak out to help save these endangered species.

Each year the spread of human habitation combined with pollution and climate change drives more species to extinction. Every nation, every community and every individual can do their part to preserve and protect the living Earth.

Promote legislation to protect endangered habitats and species; get your friends involved and use the power of your vote. You can make a difference right where you are to make our world a healthier place.

Table of Contents

Monster Birds

Legends, Myths and Marvels

The Piasa Monster

In every corner of the globe mythic tales and folklore speak of
fearsome creatures. In many of these tales giant flying monsters
swoop down to prey upon the unwary. One such creature can be seen
on the cliffs overlooking the Mississippi River near Alton, Illinois. A
fierce flying monster with dragon-like features, the Piasa Bird
monster had long been a part of local Native American folklore.

The Piasa Bird Monster-Alton, Illinois

An Ancient Terror

In 1673 French explorers Louis Jolliet and Father Jacques Marquette came to the upper Mississippi Valley and the discovered a land filled with ancient mysteries. The Illini peoples living in the valley shared tales of ancient monsters and huge earthen mounds.

The French explorers were amazed to see the images painted on the rock face. The dragon-like Piasa filled them with fear as their hosts related how the creature carried off and devoured their people in times past. The images was carved and painted on the rock in honor of the brave leader who finally slew the monster.

What could have caused the natives to create such an image? Did they have firsthand experience with some sort of giant flying creature? By the time father Marquette discovered the carving it was already hundreds of years old.

Archaeologists and historians now believe that the Piasa Bird monster and other nearby images were carved and painted by the Mississippian peoples who built Cahokia and other nearby mound sites. The original carving was destroyed in the late 19th century. The present image was painted on the rocky hillside overlooking the Mississippi River is a recreation off the original.

The Thunderbird

There may be a monster in the skies over North America. That is the consensus of many people who claim to have seen the thunderbird. From Alaska to the east coast of the United States people have reported seeing these large vulture-like birds.

While many of these sightings cannot be verified, there are incidents reported by credible military and law enforcement professionals. There have even been reports of giant flying creatures attacking humans. Where are these creatures coming from, and how can their existence be explained?

Some possible explanations for modern sightings of giant birds:

• Genetic mutation resulting in oversized members of known avian species

• A previously undiscovered species

• Mistakenly identifying known avian species due to perspective errors.

• Hoaxes and overactive imaginations

Mysterious Sightings

Some of these events are difficult to discount; in many cases the witnesses are credible military or law enforcement personnel. Other sightings were witnessed by groups of individuals. One of the most controversial reports comes from Lawndale, Illinois.

One summer evening in 1977 a group of children saw two massive birds swooping down on them. One of the birds seized a small boy in its talons and began to fly away with him. The large bird dragged the child across the yard in an attempt to fly away but dropped the violently struggling boy.

There are hundreds more tales of encounters with giant birds. Many of the witnesses are well respected and reputable community members; others are accounts related by professional military and law enforcement personnel.

One thing is certain; even one verified sighting means that monster birds do still share our skies.

A Case of Mistaken Identity

Steller's Sea Eagle

Many modern sightings can be explained away as imagination or hoax. Others may simply be a case of mistaken identity.

Steller's sea eagles sometimes wander far from their home ranges in Kamchatka and have been seen as far East as Pennsylvania in the United States.

These giant birds are one the largest living raptor species. Steller's eagles may be the source of many modern thunder bird sightings over North America.

Steller's Sea Eagle Facts

The largest of all living eagles, this giant raptor uses his keen binocular vision to pick out the food it likes. The Steller's favorite hunting strategy involves perching high up on the rocks and watching the water.

The giant raptor has a powerfully muscled body and wings up to eight feet across to allow it to dive down and seize fish and small animals. Steller's sea eagles are opportunistic feeders; they will take fish while standing in shallows, scavenge and even steal prey from other hunters.

Average Wingspan:
Up to 8 ft (2.5 m)

Average Weight:
13 to 20 lbs (6 to 9 kg)

Did you know?
The Steller's sea eagle is considered the most powerful and aggressive of its cousins, the bald eagle and the white-tailed sea eagle.

Steller's Sea Eagles are a glacial relict species that survived through several ice age cycles by staying in the Asian subarctic zone where they originated. They do not occur naturally in any other area but vagrant members of the species have been seen as far afield as Taiwan, Japan and the United States.

Thunderbirds-- Myth or Memory

Human cultures in North America have been developing for nearly 10,000 years by the time. The first European explorers saw the carvings, petro glyphs and earthen mounds and Mississippi Valley.

After the end of the last ice age human civilization in North America expanded across the continent and developed into different cultures and peoples. They would have encountered many large and sometimes frightening creatures.

Could encounters with ice age mega-beasts be the source of the bizarre creatures depicted in Native American folklore? The Thunderbird legend could well have been passed down due to encounters with real giant birds.

Was the Real Thunderbird a Teratorn?

Imagine a bird measuring 11 feet from beak to tail with a 25 foot wingspan. That is just how big the teratorn Argentavis magnificens was.(Zoo) He ruled the skies over the America's once. Officially the largest bird that ever lived, this teratorn died out about 5 million years ago but it had some big cousins in North America that lived all the way up to the end of the last ice age.

The name teratorn means wonder bird. The Pleistocene saw several of these wonder bird species and they were all larger than any flying animal alive today. Two teratorn species, Ailornis incredibilis and Teratornis merriami lived in the central and western portions of North America right up to the late Pleistocene and possibly had encounters with the earliest Americans.

Fossilized remains of teratorns have been uncovered in the La Brea tar pits in California and in several other locations across North America. The remains of teratorns have been found in human occupation sites and several teratorn nesting sites preserved in dry caves contained the bones of large mammals including mammoth and bison. Oral histories and folktales about humans encountering these giants may well be the source of the thunderbird legend.

Thunderbird Suspect Number One : Teratornis merriami

Teratornis merriami:

Range-North America
Weight-up to 40 pounds
Wingspan-12 feet
Lived during Late Pleistocene/early Holocene

The legend of the thunderbird could actually be distorted oral history relating encounters with one of North America's largest bird species. Teratornis merriami is the latest surviving member of the teratorns. The fossil record shows that the earliest Americans encountered these huge birds and may have even hunted them.

Thunderbird Suspect Number Two
Aiolornis Incredibilis

There is another possible suspect in our search for the origin of the Thunderbird legend. Ailornis incredibilis is the largest bird that ever flew in North America. This avian monster is thought to have lived in the Western portions of North America.

Fossil bones of the giant have been recovered from the La Brea Tar Pits and the Anza Borrego Park in California. The bones were recovered along with fossil remains of mammoth, saber toothed cat and other Ice Age animals.

Imagine yourself walking through the grassland with a party of Paleo-Indian hunters. Suddenly a huge shadow covers your party, blocking out the sun. A huge bird soars overhead, scanning the ground for prey animals.

The sight of the teratorn, winds spreading out over eighteen feet across fills your heart with fear and you desperately seek cover. What would you think the first time you saw this huge animal soaring across the sky? How would you describe it to your friends and family?

There is another valid reason the first Americans may have feared this creature. Some experts now believe that teratorns flew to locate prey but many have stalked and killed their prey on the ground.

We know that humans killed teratorns because their bones have been recovered from garbage middens excavated in human occupation sites across the continent. It is not known whether our ancestors were hunting the birds or killing them to protect young or weak kinsmen from attack.

Aiolornis incredibilis Facts:

• Average wingspan: 18 to 20 feet

• Average weight: 50 pounds

• Estimated range: California and Nevada

A Lasting Impact

Encounters with these monsters did make a lasting impression on Native American art and culture. Thunderbird images are a recurring theme in the folklore and art of many native cultures. A good example of this can be found in native rock carvings.

Twin Bluffs near Lisbon, Wisconsin are decorated with carvings of Thunderbirds, animals and geometric shapes. The oldest petroglyphs there were carved around 250 BC. This could well mean that early encounters with monster birds may well have been passed down in folklore and oral histories for thousands of years. (Wisconsin)

Fremont Culture petroglyphs, located east of Green River, Utah. These particular drawings are from around 600 A.D.

Relict Populations

Why did the mega-bests die out? How long did it take?

These are important questions because the first human populations in the Americas spent a great deal of time in contact with the animals that shared their world. They were hunter-gatherer people deeply in tune with their environment.

As their populations expanded across the continent they took tales of their encounters with the late Pleistocene mega-beasts with them. Whenever wandering bands of Clovis, Folsom and Paleo-Indian people met it is likely they shared food and fire together.

Young people found mates and elders shared stories that would be passed down for generations and become the folklore of modern native peoples. The monsters described in many Native American myths and legends may be great beasts from the late Pleistocene. Ancestral memories and oral history can become modern myth.

The extinction of the North American mega fauna took time. It occurred over a long span of time during which living conditions for the larger animals worsened. The climate became warmer and more humid as the glaciers receded.

The grasslands and boreal forests began to disappear and new types of plant life took hold across the continent. The changes in climate and vegetation caused habitat loss and the eventual extinction of many of the North American mega-beasts.

Declining Populations

With less food the mega-beasts suffered a population decline that increased with the advent of human hunting. The warmer, wetter climate also increased the occurrence of pandemic infectious disease.

A disease such as tuberculosis could infect and kill large numbers of animals and pass from species to species. Evidence of tuberculosis in mastodon remains indicates that pandemic disease is also a contributor to their extinction. (Trumpet)

The result is the extinction of both the giant herbivores and the animals that preyed upon them. Some species died out more quickly than others did.

Mastodons, mammoth and other mega fauna lingered on in small relict populations for several thousand years after the end of the ice age.

Many late Pleistocene species such as dire wolves and giant armadillos are likely to have been encountered by the ancient Americans. Folsom, Clovis and Paleo-Indian cultures described these encounters as part of their store of oral history.

Over time history and lore become myths and legends. Could this be how stories about monsters like the Ogopogo lake monster, Thunderbird and Bigfoot began?

Terror in the Skies over New Zealand
Haasts's Eagle

They Called it Te Hokioi

Giant flying monsters can be found in folklore and legends throughout the world. Fairy tales and fables speak of brave knights and fearsome dragons. Popular films depicting giant flying monsters in battle are part of our popular culture.

The dragons, wyverns and rocs of fable and folklore may not exist today but mankind once shared this world with real flying giants. Ancient Polynesian mariners found a real flying monster on the island of New Zealand.

Timeline-1000 AD

The First Humans Arrive in New Zealand

The first humans in New Zealand were Polynesian explorers who travelled many thousand of miles across the Pacific Ocean in outrigger canoes. They discovered an unspoiled paradise filled with exotic plants and animals.

The land was rich and filled with easily caught game animals. Giant kiwi and moa living on the island had never seen humans before and had no fear of human hunters. The Polynesian hunters soon discovered that they had something to fear themselves. Their new home was the nesting grounds of the largest and most powerful eagle of all time and anything on the ground was on this bird's menu.

The Haast's eagle soon learned added humans and their children to the menu. Now extinct, this species is the most powerful raptor ever. With an eight foot wingspan and weighing in at nearly forty pounds, this monster eagle swooped down on its prey at speeds of over fifty miles per hour. Powerful talons then ripped open flesh and crushed bones as the monster bird carried off its victim.

Maori Folklore

For hundreds of year the Maori passed down images and folklore describing Te Hokioi, the giant killer bird. The scientific community considered the stories of a giant killer eagle carrying off Maori children to be superstition or myth.

More recent DNA analysis indicates that the giant Haast's eagle and the flying monster bird of Maori legend is the same animal. (Science Daily)

Haast's Eagle Facts

• Class: Aves

• Order: Accipitriformes

• Genus: Harpagornis

• Species: H. moorei

Haast's eagles reached a total average length of over 4 feet for females and slightly smaller for males.

The bird was massively muscled for power and speed. The powerful talons combined with the impact from the eagles attack spelled a quick end for human or animal prey.

It has been estimated that the strike force delivered by this giant raptor is equivalent to being hit by a cinder block falling from atop an eight story building.

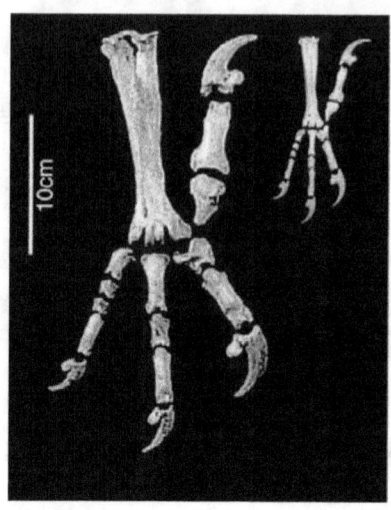

The image above is a comparison between the claws of Haast's eagle and its closest living relative, the Little Eagle. These giant talons are designed by nature for piercing flesh and bone as the bird strikes its prey. A small human or a child would have little chance of escaping an attack from this apex predator.

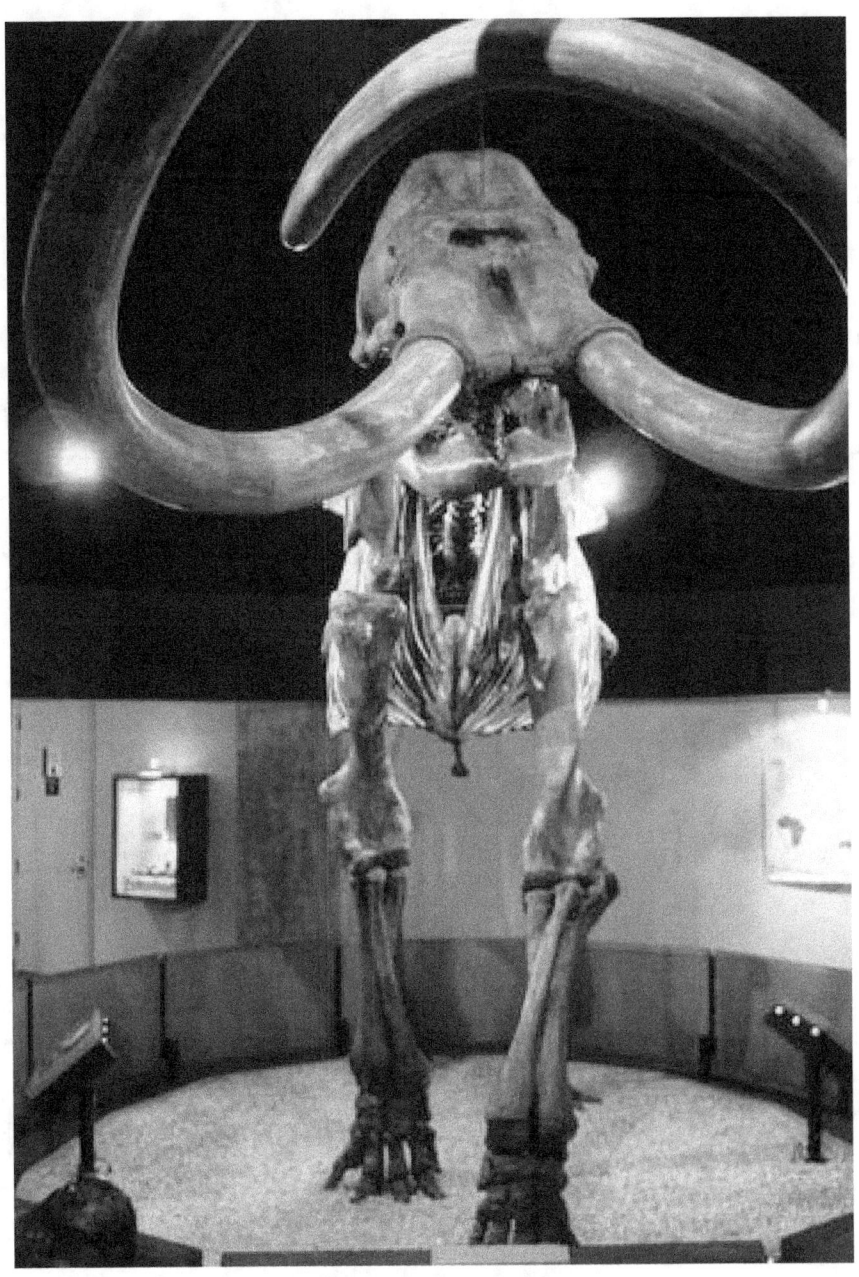

Columbia Mammoth
Attribution-ShareAlike 2.0 Generic (CC BY-SA 2.0)

A Cautionary Tale

The giant eagles of New Zealand ruled their world for many thousands of years. After humans arrived on the island that soon changed. Man shapes the world around him with disastrous impact. As in North America twelve thousand years BCE, the arrival of humans spelled the end of New Zealand's giant birds. In only a few centuries the moa and giant eagles that preyed upon them were extinct.

The story of this monster is a cautionary tale because there is an extinction event happening even as you read this book. The rapid expansion of human civilization is threatening many plant and animal species with extinction.

You can help prevent this from happening by making some simple and easy lifestyle changes. Reduce the impact you make on nature; recycle, use energy wisely and encourage your community to do the same. Small changes can make a difference if enough people care and take action.

Start fighting species loss and extinction in your own yard. Be careful to avoid using harsh chemical pesticides and herbicides that can harm the environment. Try companion planting to minimize damage from insect pests. Preserve habitat for local wildlife by planting native vegetation. Small things done by many concerned individuals can make a big reduction in our impact on the natural world.

Scaled Terrors

Sarcosuchus Imperator

"Here there be monsters"

Serpents are an ancient terror. From the earliest times our race has hated and feared reptiles. Our myths and folklore are filled with frightening scaly creatures. Eve was seduced by the serpent and Saint George fought a mighty dragon. Giant sea monsters appear in the margins of old maps, alongside the words here there be monsters.

Perhaps our ancestors possessed vivid imaginations or they were passing down ancient memories in the form of myth and legend. The stories have become exaggerated with the passage of time but in every myth there is a kernel of truth.

Scaly and alien, reptilian monsters are reported living in the great lakes of the world. Giant reptilian monsters have been sighted in Loch Ness in Scotland, Lake Champlain and Lake Okanagan in North America. Folklore and legend, myth and fairy tales going back hundreds of years document these mysterious reptilian monsters.

As frightening as tales of sea monsters may be, man has lived with giant reptile monsters in the past and still does today. Giant lizards, snakes and reptilian water monsters have shared our world for thousands of years and some still pose a threat to humans today.

Could the stories of dragons, lake monsters and sea monsters all originate from actual encounters with large, frightening animals in the distant past? We discount tales of the beast in Loch Ness and the Ogopogo as the product of overactive imaginations or misidentification.

Living Reptile Monsters

Salt Water Crocodile

Real Live Monsters

A drifting log or large sturgeon swimming on the surface of the lake might be mistaken for a monster. The Loch Ness monster may not be real but there are monsters alive today that cannot be mistaken for anything but what they are--*potential man eaters*.

Alligators and crocodiles pose a serious and growing danger to humans. These animals are being seen in urban and suburban areas more frequently as human populations expand into their natural habitat.

The American Crocodile, American Alligator and Salt Water crocodile populations are increasing rapidly due to conservation efforts. The animals are expanding their range and moving closer to human habitation as a result.

Crocodilian attacks on humans are on the rise in Africa, North America, New Guinea and Australia. Conservation efforts and reduced hunting pressure may be allowing more of the animals to live long enough to reach giant size.

Philippine Monster Croc

Some fishermen in the Philippines enlisted the aid of wildlife expert Ronnie Sumiller to land a record catch in 2011. They captured the largest saltwater crocodile on record and it only took 100 of them to land the beast.

Called Lolong, the 21 foot, 2,370 pound giant is accused of being a man eater. For nearly twenty years the villagers lived in fear as members of their community disappeared without a trace.

Giant saltwater crocodiles are known to have killed and eaten human beings in India, the Pacific and Australia. Increasing expansion of human habitation makes tragic encounters with monster crocodiles even more likely in the years to come.

Lolong will be displayed at a nearby zoological park but the locals still worry about other giants. There are reports of an even larger saltwater crocodile lurking in the nearby marshlands. (JOHN LAUINGER)

Crocodile Fact Sheet

• Crocodiles and alligators can live up to 120 years or more.

• Due to conservation efforts in the United States, Australia and Asia the crocodile population is growing quickly and more large animals are being encountered.

• Crocodiles are found in Africa, Asia, Australia and the Americas

• The largest freshwater alligator on record was caught in 1890 at Marsh Island, Louisiana. This monster gator measured an astounding 19 feet 2 inches long.

• The record for the largest crocodiles ever caught is around 21 feet but a crocodile skull on display in Orissa in India indicated the animal may have been a large as 23 feet long.

• In 2001 paleontologists unearthed the fossil remains of the largest crocodile that ever lived in the Sahara Desert. Sarcosuchus imperator reached an astounding 45 feet in length and weighed more than an elephant. Some experts think this giant feasted on a menu of giant fish and dinosaurs.(Koppes)

Gustave

One infamous Nile crocodile is the giant man eater the people in Burundi call Gustave. This monster has reportedly killed and eaten hundreds of people. Eyewitness accounts indicate that Gustave could be well over twenty feet long and may weigh over a ton.

The monster is now known world-wide thanks to a National Geographic television documentary. The story of Gustave first came to crocodile expert Brady Barr after local cichlid divers reported seeing a giant crocodile kill one of their companions.

Nile Crocodile

Crocodile attack statistics:

The Nile crocodile is responsible for more fatal attacks on humans than any other species. Over 300 attacks are reported yearly and over 60% of Nile crocodile attacks result in fatality.

The actual number of attacks is uncertain because many occur in remote areas and are not reported. The Nile crocodile is big, hungry and rapidly expanding human populations make future fatal attacks a certainty.

How big can they get?

Below is a chart showing size difference between extinct giant crocodile, living crocodile species and man. Humans are dinner sized for living monster crocs but would only be an appetizer for the Sarcosuchus. The largest living crocodiles can reach lengths of over twenty feet but they are small in comparison to extinct giants. Sarcosuchus imperator grew to nearly fifty feet in length. Paleontologists estimate their average weight to have been around eight tons.

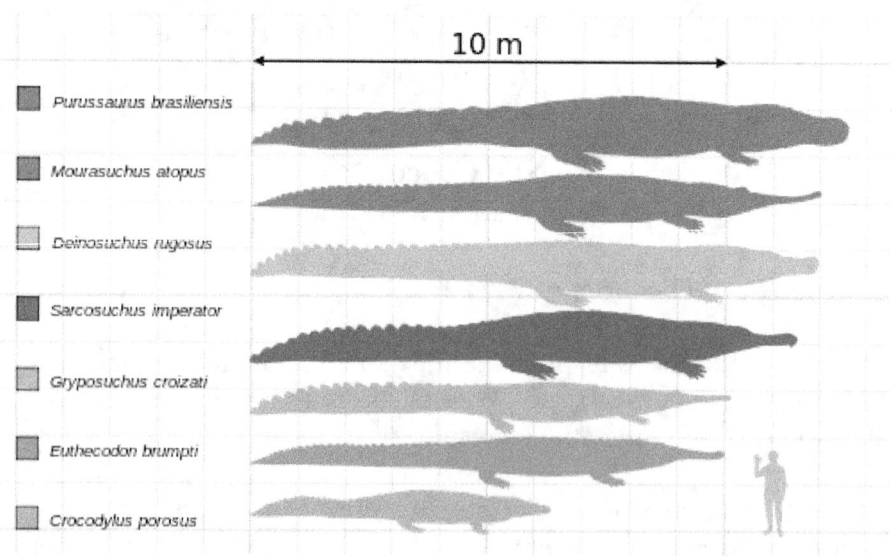

Sarcosuchus (blue) put to scale with a human and other crocodilians

Monster Monitors

Komodo Dragon
Attribution-ShareAlike 2.0 Generic (CC BY-SA 2.0)

The Komodo Dragon

Its early morning in the scrub forest and there is a hush in the air. A cold blooded killer lurks in the bush near a game trail waiting for a victim to wander by. A deer comes down the path on its way down for a morning drink and the monster tenses, ready to kill.

As the deer comes closer, 10 feet of ravenous reptile fury lunges out seizes it. Huge jaws clamp down on the hapless animal, delivering a vicious and fatal bite. The deer may escape, but its fate is sealed.

 Just one bite from the world's largest lizard can be lethal; septic bacteria in the Komodo dragon's saliva begin to kill the animal immediately. Recent studies show that this Indonesian monster's saliva contains over fifty strains of bacteria including some with anticoagulant properties. (Smithsonian, Komodo Dragon Fact Sheet)

The giant monitor lizard's keen sense of smell lets it follow the prey no matter how far it runs. One bite from this monster and anything is lunch. *Varanus komodoensis,* the Komodo dragon of Indonesia is the largest living member of the monitor lizard family and the largest lizard alive today.

Komodo dragons are indiscriminate feeders and will happily kill and eat prey as large as water buffalo. Ten feet long and weighing in at 200-300 pounds each, these monsters are cannibalistic and known man eaters. When prey is killed or scavenged many dragons gather to feed and there is little left over when the meals is done.

Terror in the Grass

Varanus komodoensis is a living reptile monster but humans have known and feared even larger lizards. To find that monster we must travel back in time to Pleistocene Australia. Say hello to Varanus priscus, the largest terrestrial lizard that ever lived. Also called megalania, this monster weighed in at over half a ton.

The aboriginal Australian people began their journey out of Africa over 70,000 years ago. They wandered across Asia, India and New Guinea before finally arriving in Australia sometime around 50,000 years ago.

Varnaus priscus

Man vs. Monster

The first Australians discovered a vast land filled with strange giant creatures. The many kangaroos, giant flightless birds and rhino sized wombats offered new sources of food for aboriginal hunters but terror lurked in the grasslands. A twenty foot long monitor lizard lurked in ambush for prey that now included humans.

Fossil evidence indicates that the earliest Australians shared the land with this monster lizard for some time before it became extinct around 40,000 years ago. Some paleontologists believe that human hunting and human induced climate change combined to drive the giant to its demise.

The use of fire by Aboriginal Australians may have changed the vegetation and helped create the type of climate found in modern day Australia.

In almost every part of the world the arrival of man altered the environment and played a role in the extinction of megafauna. Understanding this should make us be more cautious stewards of the world we live in.

Everyone can make a difference to help preserve endangered species and prevent habitat loss. (MIT) Get involved to make people in your community aware of the problem and take action to reduce our impact on nature. Save the living monsters, we don't need any more dead giants.

Invasion of the Alien Exotics

An American alligator and a Burmese python locked in a struggle to prevail in
Everglades National Park

There are some new monsters in town.

There are monsters living in the rivers of Africa and Australasia. Alligators in North America are breeding quickly and large animals up to 16 feet long now inhabit swamps and marshlands from Texas to the Carolinas. The danger from them is spreading into suburban areas in many parts of the Southeastern United States.

There were 32 serious alligator attacks on humans between 2008-2010, according to Florida Fish and Wildlife Conservation Commission. (Database: Alligator attacks in Florida) The gators now have some competition.

There may be a new contender for the title of top predator living in the Florida swamps. This new menace is an alien terror that can grow to 25 feet and will kill anything it can catch. These giants will prey on birds, deer, and small mammals. They have been known to eat alligators and can easily kill a human being.

Dangerous Discards

This alien threat did not arrive on a UFO; it came from your local pet shop. The most significant threat to the Florida ecosystem is imported exotic animals. Burmese pythons, boas and other large snakes become more trouble than their owners can handle and are released into the wild.

Conditions in the everglades are ideal these tropical constrictors. There is plenty of food and no natural predator species to restrict population growth and the population is growing. USGS authorities estimate that there are thousands of Burmese Pythons and other exotic species living in Florida's wetlands areas. (USGS)

These alien invaders pose a serious threat to both the native wildlife species and to humans. The warmer than usual winter weather experienced in the United States over the last decade further enables these animals to establish viable populations in much of Florida with the risk of these populations expanding into surrounding states as well.

Nile Monitor

Since 1990 there have been numerous sightings of the giant Nile Monitor lizard in parts of Florida. This lizard can reach up to nine feet in length and is equipped with strong jaws and powerful claws.

The swampy areas in many parts of Florida and other Southern states provide an ideal habitat for this invasive reptile species. Like the exotic snakes now found in Florida it has no natural predators in America to limit population expansion. From the pet shops to the Everglades, another imported monster seems to be here to stay.

Tegu

The South American Tegu lizard is another aggressive and troublesome alien invader. Tegus, iguanas and many other alien reptile species now call the U.S. home. Watch out, these lizards bite!

Argentine Black and White Tegu
Image Courtesy of Jami Dwyer
http://www.flickr.com/photos/jamidwyer/301717810/in/set-72157594470903897/
(en Wikipedia) [Public domain], via Wikimedia Commons

Exotic species that may pose a danger to humans in the United States:

- Snakes
  Burmese Pythons, Boas and imported venomous species

- African monitor lizards

- Tegu lizards

- Snakehead fish

- Lionfish

- Zebra Mussels

- Asian Carp

- There are also many insect, mammal and plant species that are not harmful to humans but pose a serious danger to native plant and animal species.

Alien Menace Growing

Some estimates indicate that over 25% of the plant and animal life in Florida is the result of invasive exotic species introduced into the ecosystem. Expansion of non-native species populations place native plants and animal life at risk of extinction.

Be aware of the threat and make your friends aware. It just might be your patio or back yard a 20 foot Burmese python or 10 foot African monitor lizard decides to call home. Your pets or children could be at risk from these living giant monsters.

Comfortable environmental conditions and the ever expanding suburban sprawl make future encounters between people and some of these invasive species almost a certainty. Tragic encounters with large constrictors or venomous exotic reptiles in residential areas are certain to cause problems in Florida and the other Southern states.

Act responsibly if you see an animal near your home that you do not recognize or suspect may be dangerous. Call your local animal control or fish and wildlife authorities and keep people and pets indoors and away from the animal until they arrive.

Python populations in Florida are growing rapidly. Some of these exotic snakes can grow to twenty feet and larger.

Living Monsters Dying Giants

Our journey is nearly done, now. We explored the world in search of monsters and found some true giants and some giant myths. We may never know if the thunderbird or Ogopogo really exist but know that monsters once shared our world and that some still exist.

Many of the giants man once knew are extinct now. The giants that shared the post Ice Age world with us are gone just as many species are in danger of extinction today. Then, as now, man played a role in making them die out.

Today we have a choice to help preserve the natural world and the creatures that inhabit it. Take ownership of your own environment to help protect the ecosystem. There are some easy ways that you can make a difference right at home.

Conserve water by not wasting it or dumping chemicals on the ground that can contaminate the water supply. Leaking auto coolants and chemical pesticides can cause major damage to the water and the creatures that live in it.

Chemical fertilizer can cause the death of entire marine ecosystems because it enables the rapid growth of algae. The algae uses up the oxygen in the water, kills the plants that grow there and disrupts the food chain as a result. Use organic gardening methods and companion planting instead and your garden will be healthy without harming the environment.

Find more ways you can be a better steward of the Earth. Visit the Earth Institute at Columbia University and the Center for Environmental Research and Conservation. Make a statement by making a difference where you live. (Columbia)

Don't be a dodo!

Do your part to help preserve our Earth.

Bibliography

Ancient DNA Helps Solve The Legend Of Giant Eagles. 11 January 2005.
<http://www.sciencedaily.com/releases/2005/01/050111093910.htm>.

Columbia. What You Can Do to Protect Biodiversity.
<http://blogs.ei.columbia.edu/2011/04/30/what-you-can-do-to-protect-biodiversity/>.

Database: Alligator attacks in Florida . <http://databases.sun-sentinel.com/news/broward/ftlaudGatorAttacks/ftlaudGatorAttacks_1ist.php?goto=27>.

JOHN LAUINGER. Monster saltwater crocodile, Lolong, caught in Philippines may be largest ever taken alive. 06 September 2011.
<http://articles.nydailynews.com/2011-09-06/news/30143576_1_croc-villagers-marshes>.

Koppes, Steve. "Sereno, team discover prehistoric giant Sarcosuchus imperator in African desert." 1 Nov. 2001.
<http://chronicle.uchicago.edu/011101/supercroc.shtml>.

Park, Smithsonian National Zoological. Brown(Kodiak Grizzly) Bear Fact Sheet. March 1999.
<http://nationalzoo.si.edu/Publications/ZooGoer/1999/2/fact-brown.cfm>.

Rittenour, Tammy Marie. NATIVE AMERICAN LEGEND OF THE GIANT BEAVER.
<http://www.bio.umass.edu/biology/conn.river/nalegend.html>.

Smithsonian.
<http://nationalzoo.si.edu/Publications/ZooGoer/1999/2/fact-polar.cfm>.

Trumpet, Mammoth. "Tuberculosis Found in Mastodon makes the Case for Hyperdisease in Megafauna." (2003): 2.

USAToday. "Tenn. mountains searched for bear that mauled family." (2006).

USGS. <u>Giant Constrictor Snakes in Florida: A Sizeable Research Challenge.</u> <http://www.fort.usgs.gov/FLConstrictors/>.

Wisconsin, University of. <http://www.uwlax.edu/mvac/specificsites/rockart.htm>.

Zoo, San Diego. <u>Extinct Teratorn Fact Sheet.</u> April 2009. <http://library.sandiegozoo.org/factsheets/_extinct/teratorn/teratorn.htm>.